crafting*on*the*go

beaded jewelry

crafting*on*the*go

beaded jewelry

sixth&spring
books

sixth&spring
books

233 Spring Street
New York, NY 10013

Copyright©2004 by Sixth&Spring Books

Library of Congress Cataloging-in-Publication Data

Crafting on the go! / [Editor, Trisha Malcolm]
   p. cm.
ISBN 1-931543-52-6
1. Beadwork. 2. Jewelry Making. I. Crafting on the go!

TT860.C73 2004
   745.594'2--dc22   2003067327

Manufactured in China

1 3 5 7 9 10 8 6 4 2

First Edition

contents

introduction

The fascination with jewelry and adorning oneself with it is centuries old. It seems that every culture, from the beginning of civilization, has made various forms of beaded jewelry. A trip to most museums will let you discover jewelry exhibits representing cultures and traditions from all over the earth, from ancient times to the present.

Today, young children often have their first beading experience stringing large, wooden beads on jumbo shoelace cords. Graduation to mother's or grandmother's jewelry box seeking hidden treasures comes almost as a natural progression. Glittered pony beads, embroidery floss, shiny charms, leather cords worn everywhere, seem to fascinate the younger set. As adults, we wear everything from an unpolished piece of turquoise, to a simple strand of pearls, to multi-thousand dollar diamonds! We seek out beaded treasures from the past in antique stores and flea markets, and we stare in amazement and excitement at displays in bead shops and craft stores.

It doesn't matter if it is a child's first wooden bead necklace, a bracelet made from dried beans, glittery pony beads or exotic hand-blown glass; we seem destined to gather, string and wear beads!

The ideas in this book are designed to inspire your creativity, teach basic beading techniques, pique your curiosity and desire to learn more, and illustrate the ease of creating beautiful, well designed, wearable beaded jewelry of your own.

design, color, style

There are literally hundreds of bead choices available! A simple rule is to keep it simple, especially at first. When thinking about colors, pick one you want to focus on, and stay in that family for each design. It is helpful to decide what colors and types of beads you want to use before going to the bead shop or craft store.

When deciding on bead colors, shapes and types, also determine what design style will best suit your choices. Following are brief descriptions of all the possibilities. Look for these among the designs in the book.

Symmetrical designs begin at a central point and are the same on both sides. They are balanced. The first few designs—which use the 3-5-7 concept—are symmetrical. There are others throughout the book.

Asymmetrical designs are not the same on both sides. An example of an asymmetrical design is Perfecta (page 42). The jade horse feature bead is designed to be worn on one side. The beads near the horse are larger than the beads on the opposite side.

Random designs use several different sizes, shapes and colors of beads (right). This style may seem to be the easiest, but it is important to have well thought out color selections, and interesting shapes and textures. An example of a random design is Charmed Sensation (page 46).

When all is said and done, don't forget to add your own flair—the unexpected, the extra bit of creativity that is completely yours. Don't be afraid to experiment with color and design, and enjoy the journey of discovering your own personal style.

bead types

Pipe

Melon

Tube

Round

Faceted

Bone

Art Glass

Pony

Geometric

Clay **Shaped** **Teardrop**

Chips

Charms and Novelties

Saucers or Flat

Spacers

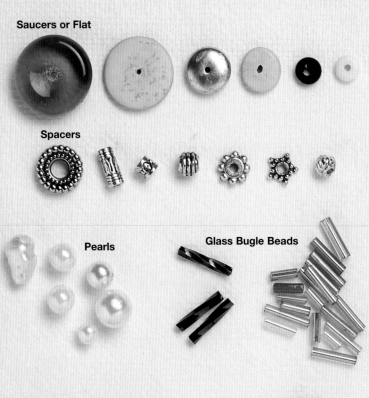

Pearls

Glass Bugle Beads

E-Beads

Seed Beads

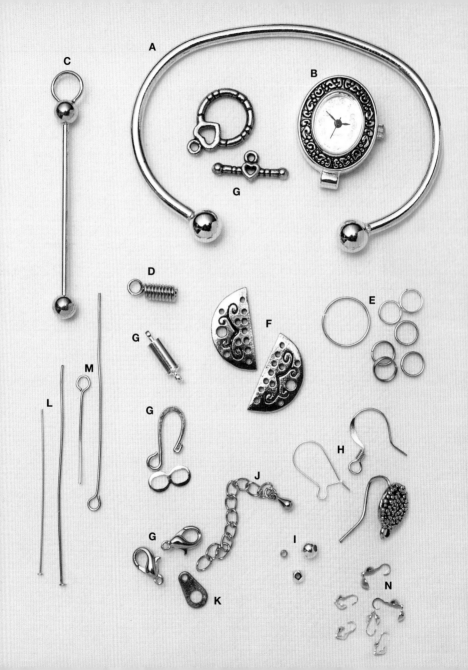

findings and other parts

"Findings" are what link together, join and finish jewelry designs. These items give designs a professional, finished look. There are many types available on the market. Purchase the best metal findings you can afford. Sterling silver and gold-filled findings are best.

A Twist End Bangle Bracelet
Sterling silver, easy to use for designing quick charm bracelets.

B Watch
Designed to hang as a necklace.

C Fancy Bead Pin
Acts as a head pin. Top unscrews, add beads and hang from necklace.

D Cord Ends
Glue and crimp over leather, suede, and thicker cord ends. Loop to hold clasp.

E Jump Rings
Wire circles with a split used as connectors.

F Multi-Strand Spacer Bar
Allows for several strands to be strung on the same piece.

G Clasps
Many types available in various sizes and shapes. A magnetic clasp has a strong magnet inside to hold jewelry on; hook and eye clasp; lobster claw clasp and spring ring clasp connect to a ring loop; toggle clasp has a bar and a loop.

H Ear Wires
Decorative and plain, gold and silver. Used for creating pierced earrings.

I Crimp Beads
Have large holes, thin walled metal beads designed to be flattened with a crimp tool or plier. Used to hold cord or wire at ends instead of knots.

J Necklace Extender Chain
Attaches to necklace to allow length adjustment.

K Tag
Acts as a loop for hooking a clasp.

L Head Pins
Look like a long straight pin only thicker with a flat or decorative end. Used to string beads or charms, loop ends and connect to jewelry. Available in different sizes.

M Eye Pins
Similar to head pins except they have a round loop on one end. You can make your own eye pins by bending wire.

N Bead Tips
Small round beads with a cup and hook. Used to link a cord-strung necklace to a clasp and conceal the knots by squeezing the bead together over the knot.

tools and other supplies

It has been said, to do the job right, you must have the right tool for the job. Part of choosing the right jewelry-making tools comes with experience. If you're a novice, however, begin small with the basics and build from there. Following are some of the possibilities, but certainly not all. All of these supplies can be found at craft stores, beading stores and on-line.

Curlers, Benders, Twisters, Grippers, Cutters, Crimpers

A Bead Crimper Tool

Has two grooves that fold a crimp bead into a tight cylinder, and round off rough edges.

B Nipper Tool

Cuts stringing wire, craft wire, bead cords, elastic cord. Not recommended for memory wire. Other wire cutters will work on wire only. Thread snips, scissors or clippers will cut bead stringing cord.

C Chain Nose Pliers

Close bead tips, crimp, shape, and bend. Also will get into small places. Inside tips are smooth so as not to mark soft wire. Needle nose or round nose pliers also will work.

D 3-in-1 Jewelry Maker's Tool

Wraps, curves, and cuts wire. An alternative to chain nose, round nose pliers or cutters. It is helpful to have more than one needle nose, chain nose or round nose pliers so one can be used for holding while the other twists or wraps.

Other Supplies

E Tweezers

Pick up beads, hold small items.

F Beeswax

Conditions and softens thread and makes it easier to thread small needles. Helps thread glide through beads, prevents threads and cords from fraying.

G Beading Needles

For use with beading cords and threads in assorted sizes. Collapsible eye needles, twisted beading needles and big eye beading needles are popular choices.

Stringing Materials

H Greek Leather Cord

Flexible and long lasting round cord with a smooth finish and supple texture. Usually can be found in black, brown, and natural.

I Beading Cords

Choose a size that will pass through beads four times. Sizes are indicated by a number or letter; the lower the number or letter, the thinner the cord. When using cord, always double it.

(continued on page 16)

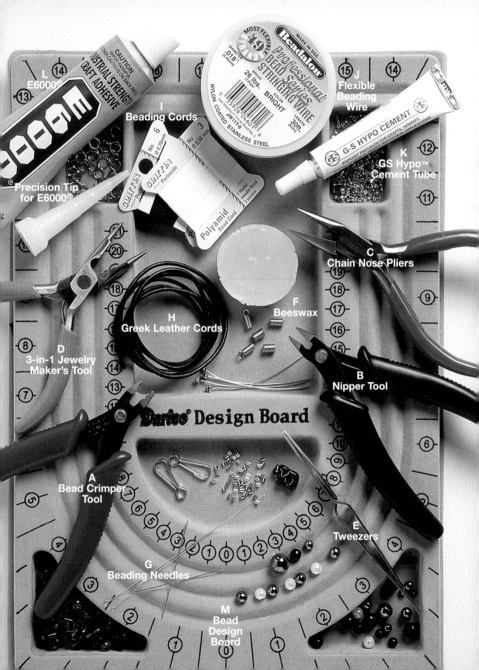

L E6000® INDUSTRIAL STRENGTH CRAFT ADHESIVE

I Beading Cords

J Flexible Beading Wire

Precision Tip for E6000®

K GS Hypo™ Cement Tube

C Chain Nose Pliers

F Beeswax

H Greek Leather Cords

D 3-in-1 Jewelry Maker's Tool

B Nipper Tool

Darice® Design Board

A Bead Crimper Tool

E Tweezers

G Beading Needles

M Bead Design Board

(continued from page 14)

100% Silk—Soft, drapes well. Large color selection.

Poly-Nylon—Stronger than silk and twice as strong as ordinary nylon. Knots easily. Large color selection.

High Performance (HP)—Very strong, won't tear, or break in the knot. White only. Cannot be dyed.

J Flexible Beading Wire

Beadalon® 49 Strand—Soft, flexible, nylon coated and strong. Works with ceramic, metal, glass, stone, seed beads, fresh water pearls. Knots easily. Flexible beading wire is available in several brands, sizes and colors. The more inner wires in a cord, the more flexible and kink-resistant it is.

Glues

K GS Hypo™ Cement

Dries clear, has a precision applicator, safe for all surfaces. Will not bond to fingers. Works on plastic, glass, metal and ceramic beads.

L E6000®

Bonds tight, dries clear, acid free. Comes with precision tip. Do not secure knots with clear nail polish, as it will cause cords to become brittle and break. Other clear drying craft glues will also work.

Miscellaneous

M Bead Design Board

Provides channels to lay out beads, and compartments to hold beads and findings. Hint: if a bead design board is not available, lay out a towel to hold beads in place while designing.

Bead Size Chart

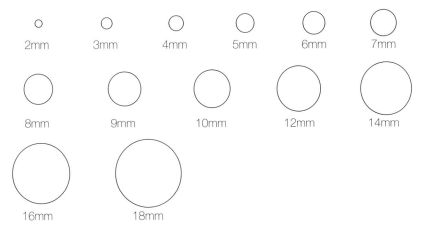

| 2mm | 3mm | 4mm | 5mm | 6mm | 7mm |

| 8mm | 9mm | 10mm | 12mm | 14mm |

| 16mm | 18mm |

Cord and Wire Size Chart

Beadalon® Wire Diameters

inches	mm	actual size
.010	0.25	
.012	0.30	
.013	0.33	
.015	0.38	
.018	0.46	
.020	0.51	
.021	0.53	
.024	0.61	
.026	0.66	

Bead Cord Widths

	inches	mm	actual size
No. 0	.012	0.30	
No. 1	.014	0.35	
No. 2	.018	0.45	
No. 3	.020	0.50	
No. 4	.024	0.60	
No. 5	.026	0.65	
No. 6	.028	0.70	
No. 8	.032	0.80	

3 beads

Black leather cord

One feature bead or button

Two silver spacer beads

Cord spring ends and clasp

Glue

5 beads

Black leather cord

Two silver tube spacer beads
To achieve balance, each two spacer beads should be the same.

Two spacer beads

One feature bead or pendant

Cord spring ends and clasp

Glue

7 beads

Black woven cord

Four silver spacer beads (identical)

Two black pony beads

One feature bead or pendant

necklaces— easy as 3–5–7!

Begin your beading experience with the 3–5–7 design concept. See how easy it is to create nice looking, symmetrical designs with just a few beads.

3 beads

1 Cut cord to desired length. Fold in half to determine middle.

2 Thread silver spacer bead, feature bead, spacer bead on to cord.

3 Glue cord spring ends on each end of cord. Attach clasp.

5 beads

1 Follow steps above, stringing two of the spacers on cord, feature bead, two spacers.

2 Finish as above.

7 beads

1 Cut cord to desired length adding 4" (10.2cm) for ending. Fold cord in half. Pull folded end through hanging hole on feature bead. Pull loose ends through cord loop and pull cord close to top of bead, adjust and tighten. This is known as a lark's knot.

2 Thread one pony bead between two silver spacer beads on each cord.

3 If desired, finish ends by tying a knot instead of adding a closure. Trim excess.

bracelets—easy as 1–3–5!

materials

1 bead

One feature bead

Approx. 37 turquoise chips

Glue

3 beads

One feature bead

Two accent beads

Approx. 25 green agate chips

Glue

5 beads

One feature bead

Four accent beads, two of each size and style

Approx. 30 apple coral chips

Glue

Apply the same easy design concept with necklaces for three easy bracelets. Use Beadalon® Elasticity™ 0.5mm clear beading cord for all three projects, along with a collapsible eye beading needle. When working with beads with small holes, make sure cord and needles fit through the smallest hole.

1 bead

1 Measure wrist. Cut cord longer than needed for ease in beading and knotting.

2 String turquoise chips on cord. String feature bead on one side of cord. Tie cord in double knot. Add dot of glue to knot and work knot into feature bead hole.

3 beads

1 Cut cord longer than wrist as noted above.

2 String bead chips on cord and center. On one side of cord, string one accent bead, feature bead, accent bead.

3 Tie double knot close to beads, pulling tightly. Trim excess cord, add drop of glue to knot and work knot into hole of one of the larger beads.

5 beads

1 Follow same steps as with bracelets above, adding one each of accent beads on each side of feature bead. Finish as above.

for each pair

Two decorative ear wires

Two decorative tip head pins

3 beads

One teardrop bead

Two smaller accent beads

5 beads

One teardrop bead

Four accent beads in varying sizes and shapes

7 beads

One teardrop bead

Six accent beads in varying sizes and shapes

Chain nose pliers

earrings—easy as 3–5–7!

Earrings are fun accessories to add to your wardrobe, and all three of these dangles are easy to make. Designing to achieve an attractive, balanced look is easy too, when you apply the 3–5–7 design theory.

1 bead

1 For one teardrop bead, thread the decorative head pin through one bead, loop the top using round nose pliers and hang on the ear wire loop. Repeat for second earring.

3, 5 or 7 beads

1 When adding three or five or seven beads to the head pin, it is important to consider size, color, and balance. The earrings in the opposite photograph are good examples of adding more beads and achieving good balance and color coordination.

beading style: symmetrical
with feature bead
finished size: 28"(71cm)

**One natural turquoise
nugget**

**26 red wooden tube
beads**

**26 red porcelain pony
beads**

**Four round 5mm red
wood beads**

**Four round 5mm
turquoise beads**

**Eight silver tube spacer
beads**

**Two silver flat spacer
beads**

**Two silver beads larger
than the hole on feature
bead**

One 2"(5.1cm) head pin

**32"(76.5cm) Beadalon®
Greek Leather Cord
in brown**

**Two Beadalon® 1.8mm
silver cord ends**

**One Beadalon® Greek
clasp**

Chain nose pliers

southwest sunset

**There is something soothing about wearing a natural
"gem of the earth," and turquoise is a lovely, timeless
choice. This design is easy to accomplish and makes
a fashionable statement with any outfit.**

1 On head pin, string one silver bead, feature nugget,
silver bead. Loop head pin with chain nose pliers.
On beading board, lay out small beads on each side
of nugget in the following manner: red bead, silver
spacer tube, turquoise bead, silver spacer tube, red
bead, silver spacer tube, turquoise bead, silver spacer
tube, flat silver spacer.

2 Beginning with porcelain pony bead, string
remaining beads, alternating tube beads and pony
beads.

3 Finish off each end with Beadalon® cord ends and
Greek clasp.

dragonfly
hat pin

materials

**One Darice® Silver 4½"
(11.5cm) hat pin with
end clutch**

**One carved bone
dragonfly
[or any other feature
bead(s)]**

**One 8mm, 9mm or 10mm
round bead**

**Four assorted shapes
silver spacer beads**

Glue

**Hat pins are terrific accessories…and not just for
hats! Take this idea and add your imagination to
create a one-of-a-kind accessory to spark up your
lapel, collar, scarf and more!**

1 Choose a favorite feature bead and build your pin
around that. Compliment the colors in the feature
with the smaller beads, and the rest is up to your
vivid imagination.

2 Thread beads on pin, beginning at top. Add a drop
of glue inside last bead. If bead is larger than hat
pin, carefully "stuff" inside of bead with a small
amount of beading thread. Add some glue to both
ends of bead to secure.

black-eyed beauty

materials

Three 14"(35.5cm) strands brown Greek leather cord
Measure wrist and add approx. 8"(20.3cm) for working.

Three 9.5mm black glass eye beads

Two black pony beads

One flat, oval brown iridescent bead

One 3mm brown bead

16"(40.6cm) 20 gauge silver Beadalon® Colourcraft wire

One silver jump ring

One silver head pin

Five 5mm silver spacer beads

The Beadery® 3-in-1 Jewelry Maker's Tool

Try this different twist on a leather bracelet. Greek leather holds its shape and is easy to work with. The beautiful and interesting black-eye beads add a bit of mystery to this simple bracelet. Try these beads and this design in different colors too! It will look great with jeans or other casual outfits.

1 On head pin, string 3mm brown bead, one glass eye bead, one silver spacer bead. Loop end of head pin and trim excess using a snipper tool. Attach jump ring through loop and close. Set aside.

2 Cut leather cord as noted above. Hold three pieces together at one end. Loop all three cords and while holding with one hand, wrap silver wire around once, string jump ring with eye bead onto wire and continue wrapping tightly several times to secure loop. If needed, work beaded charm to side of bracelet. Bend wire ends in to avoid snagging. Set aside.

3 Cut 8"(20.3cm) length of wire. String black pony bead, silver spacer bead, black glass eye bead, flat oval bead, silver spacer, black glass eye bead, silver spacer, black pony bead. Center beads on wire.

4 Feed each wire end back through the pony bead, holding tightly with fingers and pulling wire and adjusting beads so they are still close together. Wire should end up on top of pony bead.

5 Wrap wire four times around middle leather cord on one end. Loop leather cord around beads once, beginning under the beads, cross over the top center bead and then to the underside of the pony bead. Wrap wire four times around the middle cord. Pull the two outside cords together with the middle cord and wrap all three cords four more times. Snip wire. Bend wire in to avoid snagging. With remaining wire, wrap the other side of three cords together four times.

6 Adjust center cord and beads on wire and slightly curve to wrist shape. When satisfied, re-measure bracelet and tie a loose knot on the opposite end of the loop made in Step 2, leaving a 5"(12.7cm) tail. Feed tail pieces through the center of the knot, pulling tightly to secure. Clip ends.

Note

Looped end should be approximately a ½"(1.3cm) opening and the knot will also be about ½"(1.3cm).

Two silver ear wires

Two silver head pins

Round nose pliers

Chain nose pliers

Wire nippers

aventurine (green)

**Two 10mm round
aventurine beads**

**Two 8mm dotted silver
spacers**

carnelian (red)

**Four 6mm round
carnelian beads**

**Two 6mm floral ring
silver spacers**

amethyst (lavender)

Eight amethyst chips

**Two 8mm cylindrical
silver spacers**

three's company

**Any one of these three easy-to-achieve designs will
definitely brighten your smile! Whip them up in a hurry
and wear them out that night, or give a pair or two as
a handmade gift. Choose different colors and spacers
and go for even more looks.**

For each pair

1 String beads as shown on each head pin. At top of
head pin, use round nose pliers to make a loop.
Wrap extra wire around head pin just below loop.
Use chain nose pliers to press wire end in toward
wrapped area to prevent snagging.

2 Attach loop to ear wire.

Tip

Natural beads will often vary in size and color.
When choosing beads, lay them out and compare to
make sure both earrings are a very close match.

materials

beading style: symmetrical
with feature bead

finished size: 32"(82.4cm)

**24"(61cm) Beadalon®
natural suede cord
(3.2mm)**

**24"(61cm) Beadalon®
19 0.33mm silver
beading wire**

**One carved bone feature
bead**

**Four medium glass or
wood tube beads**

11 7mm silver ball beads

Approx. 10 red coral chips

26 natural color E-beads

10 silver tube spacers

**4"(10cm) of 20 (0.81mm)
gauge silver wire**

Two silver crimp beads

Eight silver E-beads

**Darice® 2½"(6.35cm)
silver Steel Fancy
Bead Pin**

**Two silver suede cord
ends**

Silver lobster claw clasp

Chain nose pliers

Wire nippers

Glue

**Now the perfect solution to hanging a feature bead
without bending and looping wire! All you need is the
Darice® Fancy Bead Pin.**

1 Place feature bead on Fancy Bead Pin. Set aside.

2 Cut suede cord in half. On each cord, loop one end
and tightly wrap silver wire around three or four
times to secure. Clip wire end and bend in.

3 Loop one end of silver beading wire through leather
loop and secure with crimp bead.

4 Thread beads on beading wire in this order: tube
spacer bead, E-bead, silver spacer bead, glass tube
bead, silver spacer, E-bead, silver tube spacer, E-
bead, silver ball, silver spacer bead, 3 coral chips, E-
bead, silver ball, E-bead, silver tube spacer, E-bead,
silver spacer, glass tube bead, silver spacer, E-bead,
silver tube spacer, E-bead, silver ball, E-bead, two
coral chips, E-bead, silver ball, E-bead, silver spacer
tube, E-bead, silver ball. This should be center of
necklace. Thread feature bead on pin through cord
and repeat above for other side of necklace.

5 Loop beading wire through second leather loop and
secure as in Step 3.

6 Determine desired length for suede cord and clip
excess. Place drop of glue inside of a suede cord
end. Place suede end into finding and crimp closed.
Repeat on other cord. Attach lobster claw clasp to
ends to finish.

34

materials

beading style: double strand, symmetrical
finished size: 20"

One feature bead
Six 6mm round turquoise beads
Approx. 24 turquoise chips
Approx. 216 turquoise-colored seed beads
12 8mm turquoise-colored washer beads
12 6mm silver spacers
10 5mm silver spacers
12 1mm silver coil spacers
One turquoise E-bead
Two 4x2mm turquoise heishe beads
19"(48.4cm) length 0.38mm Beadalon® 19 flexible beading wire
18"(45.9cm) length of 1mm diameter tan leather cord
One fancy bead pin
Two 4mm silver jump rings
One 8mm silver jump ring
Silver toggle clasp
Chain nose pliers
Crimper tool

turquoise double delight

This delicate design can showcase your own personal taste. Instead of a bone bead as shown, choose a small cross or an interesting medallion for the center. This is also an easy style to change colors and beads to achieve a completely different look.

1 String turquoise heishe bead, feature bead and other turquoise heishe bead onto fancy head pin. String an E-bead onto an 8mm jump ring and attach it to top loop of head pin.

2 Thread leather cord through 8mm jump ring and adjust so bead is in the center. One one side of bead, leave ¾"(1.9cm) then string silver coil spacer. Use chain nose pliers to flatten one or two loops to hold spacer in place. String two turquoise washers and another silver coil. Again, flatten one or two loops of coil to hold spacer in place.

3 String two more beaded units on the same side of necklace, about 2"(5.1cm) apart. String a coil spacer onto the end of necklace and flatten one or two loops to secure. Bend up one coil at opposite end forming a loop. Attach loop to the 4mm jump ring on one half of the clasp. Repeat the beading pattern and clasp attachment on the other half of the necklace.

4 String beads on wire in the following pattern: 5mm silver spacer, eight turquoise chips, 5mm silver spacer, 1"(2.5cm) of seed beads, 6mm silver spacer, 6mm round turquoise bead, 6mm silver spacer, 1"(2.5cm) of seed beads, *5mm silver spacer, 4 turquoise chips, 5mm silver spacer, 1" (2.5cm) of seed beads, 6mm silver spacer, 6mm round turquoise bead, 6mm silver spacer, 1"(2.5cm) of seed beads*. Repeat pattern between *'s once more.

5 String a crimp bead, place the end through a 4mm jump ring and place it back into the crimp bead. Use a crimper tool to crimp the bead. Cut off any excess. Attach the jump ring to half of the clasp. String on 1"(2.5cm) of seed beads, 6mm silver spacer, 6mm round turquoise bead, 6mm silver spacer and 1"(2.5cm) of seed beads. Continue to repeat the beading pattern between the *'s on the other half of the necklace.

ruby red lariat

materials

beading style: ends are random

finished size: 30"(76.5 cm) w/o toggle ring

One yard (1m) Beadalon®49 0.33mm Silver Professional Bead Stringing Wire

Assorted red beads: one teardrop, three 8mm balls, 21 red glass E-beads, approx. 370 red seed beads

(16 seed beads per inch)

Silver beads: 18 crimp beads, 13 tube spacer beads, three flat spacer beads, one 3mm silver ball, one flower edge spacer bead

One silver toggle loop

One silver head pin

Chain nose pliers

Crimper tool

Nipper tool

This little lariat will surely wrangle in some compliments! Quick and easy to make, it's something you'll want to create in different colors. Make it a little longer so you can wrap it around your neck a few times!

1 String silver bead, red 8mm ball, flower edge spacer, red teardrop, silver tube spacer and red E-Bead on head pin. Loop end of head pin with chain nose pliers. Set aside.

2 Loop one end of wire through toggle loop. Thread crimper bead on wire, pull wire end through crimp bead and crimp closed. Trim excess.

3 Thread red beads, crimp beads and spacers in a pleasing design for about 5"(12.7cm).

4 Continue threading red seed beads for about 21"(53.6cm).

5 Repeat design pattern with red and silver beads and additional seed beads for about 4"(10cm).

6 Crimp other end closed. Trim excess and feed end back through several beads to secure. Adjust as necessary to make sure all beads are distributed evenly.

perfecta

A long, stylish necklace is the perfect way to begin your beading experience. The jade horse is a dramatic statement, but search for other types of feature beads to suit your personal style. Be sure to lay out all the beads and try different arrangements to find the design you like best. A bead design board is helpful for this project. Pay attention to shape, size and color. Keep the weight of the feature bead in mind. Make sure to have an equal weight of beads opposite the feature bead so the necklace stays balanced.

materials

beading style:
asymmetrical/random

finished length:
36"(91.5cm)

Jade carved horse
(or other feature bead)

Assorted beads
Approximate number of beads required: 200: pearls, green glass, silver carved, silver spacers in all sizes, assorted green, white and grey round beads.

Beadalon®/Griffen™ No. 4 HP (High Performance) bead cord

Scotch tape

Glue

1 Take all the beading cord off the card. If it is kinked from being on the card, wet it and hang with weights on each end. Let dry overnight.

2 Tape a piece of scotch tape on one end of the cord to avoid beads slipping off while stringing. Once you have laid out your design, begin stringing the beads.

3 When all beads are in place and you are satisfied with the final design, remove tape from end of beading cord. Tie a double knot in cord and trim excess. Add a drop of glue to knot and slide knot under a bead to conceal.

Hint

If some bead holes seem too large for the cord, place a small dot of glue inside bead. Cut a small piece of cord and stuff inside bead. Be careful not to over-glue or over stuff the cord.

gifts of the sea

Nothing makes a statement of elegance better than a perfect string of pearls. A lovely duo of mother-of-pearl medallions to the center adds an extra touch of good taste and personal style.

materials

finished size: 20"(51.0cm)

Approx. 75 6mm fresh water pearls (optional: small spacer beads for between each pearl)

One 50mm mother of pearl medallion with hole in top

One 30mm mother of pearl medallion with hole in top

One 12mm sterling silver jump ring

Beadalon®/Griffin™ Polyamid bead cord, No. 4, 0.60mm diameter, white

Two silver Beadalon® bead tips

One silver barrel clasp

Glue

1 Before beginning, unwind all beading cord from card. If cord is slightly kinked from being on the card, lightly wet it and hang it over a door or hook with weights on both ends. Let dry and cord will be ready for beading. Note also that Beadalon® Griffin™ cord comes with its own needle.

2 Determine desired necklace length. At opposite end from needle on cord, thread barrel clasp and crimp tube onto cord. Knot cord and place knot inside bead tip cup with a dot of glue. Close.

3 String desired number of pearls on cord. Attach the other end of barrel clasp as in Step 1.

4 Open silver jump ring and put on large disk and smaller disk on top. Hang at center of necklace, close jump ring securely and gently place ring between center pearls. If desired, add a drop of glue on cord and jump ring to secure in place.

beading style: random
finished size: 20"(56cm)

Selected beads, charms and buttons in varying sizes and shapes

Photo examples: carved bone flower, locket, natural stone, wooden beads, glass beads, large round amber bead, Chinese coin

Variety of spacer beads

Up to three jump rings for each charm

Three colors of embroidery floss, each 6"(15.3cm)

Two, 4mm sterling silver crimp beads (tassle ends)

Two 1.5mm crimp beads (necklace ends)

One clasp

24"(61cm) Beadalon® 49 Strand Bead Stringing Wire, 0.46mm

Beading board

Nipper tool

Chain nose pliers

Glue

charmed sensation

The beads and charms for this necklace can come from many places—antique jewelry, broken earrings and even your button box!

1 Cut a 24"(61cm) length of wire. Set aside.

2 Determine feature bead and place on beading board. Continue randomly sorting beads on each side of feature bead. After all the beads are laid out in a pleasing manner, place a "sub-feature bead" of similar size on each side of feature bead.

3 Continue placing and balancing the charms on both sides of necklace.

4 To each charm, depending on size and length, add jump rings. If additional length is needed, add another jump ring.

5 To make embroidery floss tassel, between thumb and index finger, twist floss together. Hold twisted section tightly and feed end through silver crimp bead. Crimp bead closed to hold twist. Re-twist the other end and repeat with other crimp bead.

6 If feature bead is a stone (as shown), thread wire or cord through hole in stone, knot tightly at back and glue knot to secure to back. Glue small glass bead to front of stone to cover hole. Feed jump ring through top of bead. Before closing jump ring, add tassel. Close jump ring, knot tassel. Secure knot.

7 Finish ends with crimp beads and clasp.

hoop dreams

for each pair

- **Two sterling silver ear wires**

- **Two 12mm silver jump rings**

- **Beadalon® Ring Remembrance™ stainless steel memory wire**

- **Four 12mm charms**
  Shown are Chinese coins.

- **Eight silver flower spacer beads**

- **Eight 3mm silver balls**

- **Eight 3mm silver spacer beads with different design from above**

- **Four silver flat star shaped spacer beads**

- **Two silver decorative beads, not larger than 14mm**

- **Round nose pliers**

- **Wire nippers**

- **Glue**

Dangling earrings are great fun and add a special "zing" to your look. Because these are strung on stainless steel memory wire, they will hold their shape perfectly.

For each earring

1 To create largest circle, pull ring size memory wire away from its coil, stretching it slightly so that it is about twice the size of the ring coil, or about 1"(2.5cm) across. Snip it with wire cutters. Gently pull and shape it until it is the correct size. Make each hoop slightly smaller than the first.

Hint

Memory wire is just that, it remembers where it was and wants to return to that shape, so working with it takes a little effort. Work carefully so it doesn't snap back at you!

2 String beads on each wire hoop as shown in photo.

3 Adjust beads on each wire loop so bead is covering wire opening. Glue center bead to wire at that point and if needed, place small amounts of glue to secure other beads in place.

kicky anklets

Anklets are fun to wear and these are so easy, you will want to make dozens! Give them away to your friends, or wear several at a time! It's a matter of choosing your favorite beads and charms and stringing them on the ready-to-go silver ball chains.

materials

for each anklet

One 9"(22.9cm) silver ball chain with clasp

Beader's choice bead selection. Shown are: colored pony beads, silver washers, colored washers, silver beads, glass beads. Keep in mind that ball chain must fit through bead holes.

1 String bead assortment on chain in desired arrangement and close clasp. Voilà!

chunky charmer

materials

All supplies provided by
Blue Moon Beads, Inc.

**Silver blank charm
bracelet with 32 links
and clasp**

**Four 11mm art glass
bead squares**

**Four 11mm turquoise
chunks**

Four silver charms
("believe", sun, shell,
heart)

**Four 4mm round
turquoise beads**

**Four 6mm dotted silver
spacers**

**Four 6mm cylindrical
silver spacers**

**Four 8mm dotted silver
spacers**

Four 10mm silver leaves

Six silver bells

19 8mm silver jump rings

Four silver eye pins

12 silver head pins

36 matte red E-beads

Round nose pliers

Chain nose pliers

Wire nippers

Charm bracelets are back! They look complicated, but you'll be pleased to see how easily this one comes together. Everyone will wonder where you got it!

1 String the following beads onto a head pin: 5mm silver spacer, square glass bead, 6mm dotted spacer, 6mm turquoise bead. Make a wrapped loop to attach charm to second link on bracelet. Repeat for three more charms and attach one to the 10th, 18th and 26th links.

2 String a leaf bead onto the loop of an eye pin. String a red E-bead and a 4mm turquoise bead onto the pin. Make a wrapped loop to attach the charm to the 4th link. Repeat for three more charms and attach one to the 12th, 20th and 28th links.

3 String two E-beads, a cylindrical spacer and an E-bead onto a head pin. Make a wrapped loop to attach the charms to the same links as the beaded leaf charms.

4 String a favorite silver charm onto an 8mm jump ring; repeat for four charms. Place a red E-bead on the ring on each side of the charm. Attach a charm to the 5th, 13th, 21st and 29th links.

5 String a turquoise chunk and an 8mm dotted spacer onto a head pin. Make a wrapped loop to attach the charm to the 6th link. Repeat Step 3 for three more charms and attach one to the 14th, 22nd, and 30th links.

6 String two silver bells onto a jump ring; repeat for three charms. Attach one to the 8th, 16th and 24th links.

7 String a red E-bead onto each of the remaining jump rings. Attach one jump ring to each blank link on the bracelet.

finished size: longest
strand is 20"(51cm),
middle strand is
18"(45.8cm), shortest
strand is 15"(38.2cm)

**Three Blue Moon Beads
Czech glass art beads:
10mm white tube, 10mm
red ball, 12mm blue tube**

Two red seed beads

**Two purple/blue
iridescent seed beads**

**Two 6mm turquoise
colored beads**

**Two 6mm dark blue
beads**

**Two 6x3mm medium blue
faceted disc beads**

**1½ yards (1.4m)
Beadalon® 7 0.38mm
purple flexible bead
stringing wire**

**Two silver double-cup
bead tips**

Two crimp beads

**Two 6mm silver jump
rings**

Spring ring clasp

Crimper tool

Wire nippers

Glue

jazzy glass bead triple strand

**Perfect for beginner beaders, this easy-to-make project
demonstrates how to combine a few bright colors on
some pretty purple wire to create one of the hottest
looks in jewelry.**

1 Cut one wire 17"(43.3cm), one 20"(51.0cm) and one
22"(56.0cm).

2 String 22" wire: blue seed bead, dark blue 6mm
bead, blue glass tube bead, dark blue 6mm, blue
seed bead. Set aside.

3 String 20" wire: red seed bead, 6mm turquoise bead,
red ball glass bead, 6mm turquoise bead, red seed
bead. Set aside.

4 String 17" wire with blue faceted disc bead, white
glass bead, blue faceted disc bead.

5 Move all beads to the center of each of the wires.
Even up the three wires on one side of necklace and
thread a crimp bead onto all three wires. Crimp the
wires together. Repeat on other side. Trim excess
wire above crimp bead.

6 Place a drop of glue inside the bead tip cup. Place
crimped end into bead tip and glue. Close bead tip.
Repeat on other side.

7 Attach jump ring to bead tip on each side and
attach spring ring clasp on one side.

Olive jade donut

Chinese red cinnabar donut

Three 8mm red glass pony beads

Three 5mm dark red porcelain pony beads

Three 8mm lime green glass pony beads

Three 14mm flat, round silver beads

Five 8mm silver beads

Seven 6mm silver beads

One 4mm silver bead

One 8mm decorated silver spacer bead

One 7mm silver tube spacer bead

Two tube decorated silver beads

Four 5mm silver crimp beads

Two 3.5mm silver spring spacers

One 5mm silver jump ring

One silver head pin

One silver toggle clasp

Black elastic beading cord

Double wrist measurement plus 8"(20.3cm).

Lime green embroidery floss, narrow ribbon or cord

Chain nose pliers

Glue

limeade charmer

Bracelets are fun and quick to make. This one has many interesting "charming" elements, and the color combination makes it a neon delight!

1 On silver head pin, bead 4mm silver bead. Place silver tube bead inside hole in cinnabar donut and thread head pin through both tube bead and cinnabar, 8mm decorated spacer bead. Loop end of head pin. Place silver jump ring through loop on head pin.

2 Fold beading cord in half. Thread folded end through hole in jade donut, through jump ring holding dangle charm made in Step 1, and pull loose ends of cord through cord loop (lark's knot).

3 String both cords through 6mm silver bead. String one spring spacer on one of the cords. Loop that cord through the toggle clasp and through the spring spacer. Pull cord, spring spacer and toggle close to first bead. Press spacer tightly to hold cord.

4 String both cords through a 6mm silver bead, red pony bead, lime green pony bead. Knot the two cords together tightly. Add a drop of glue to the knot and work the green pony bead so the knot is inside the bead.

5 Continue stringing on one cord in the following manner: Flat silver bead, large red pony bead, 8mm silver bead, 4mm silver bead, decorative silver tube bead, 4mm silver bead, 8mm silver bead, small red pony bead, lime green pony bead, flat silver bead, large red pony bead, 8mm silver bead, 4mm silver bead, decorative silver tube bead, 4mm silver bead, 8mm silver bead, 4mm silver bead, small red pony bead, lime green pony bead, flat silver bead, large red pony bead. (Make adjustments according to wrist size.)

6 Thread spring spacer on cord, loop cord through other toggle clasp and thread end of cord through spring spacer. Press spacer tightly to hold cord. Thread cord end back through beads.

7 To make embroidery floss tassels, tightly twist or braid embroidery floss, securing with a crimp bead on end. Make two or three tassels and hang on cord with lark's knot.

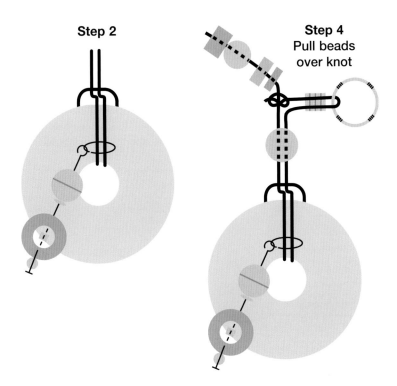

Step 2

Step 4
Pull beads
over knot

stripe it up

materials

beading style: random
finished size: approx.
16"(40.8cm)

**18"(45.9cm) black Greek
leather cord**

**Assorted Blue Moon
Beads art glass large
cane beads (total 13 for
this design) in round,
triangle, square, and
flower shapes**

**14 6mm black porcelain
pony beads**

**Two 1.8mm silver Greek
cord ends**

One Greek clasp

Chain nose pliers

Glue

**Stringing bright and shiny glass beads on a black cord
is easy and striking, and great fun for kids of all ages.
The length of this piece is your own choice, since it
will look fabulous as a choker or longer. Plus, it's so
quick to do—after a little planning, you'll be wearing it
in no time flat!**

1 Alternating shapes and colors, arrange art glass
beads until you find a pleasing pattern.

2 Beginning with a pony bead, string glass bead, pony
bead, glass bead, pony bead, etc., until all beads are
strung. End with a pony bead.

3 Cut leather cord to desired length. Glue Greek cord
ends on and attach clasp.

fast and fun
charm bracelets

A neat-looking sterling silver bangle bracelet makes this design easy and fun to create by you, and a great project for the younger set to design and make on their own. Plus, they're easy to remake whenever the mood strikes you!

materials

Darice® Twist End Silver Bangle Bracelet

Charms and beads as desired
Shown are: silver pony beads, silver spacer beads and some fun charms from Blue Moon Beads.

1 Unscrew the end ball and string on as many beads and charms as you like in the design of your choice. Screw the end back on and enjoy!

aventurine chandelier earrings

materials

24 4mm round aventurine beads

Six 6mm round aventurine beads

Four aventurine chips

Six silver cylindrical beads

Eight 5mm silver spacers

Two 6mm dotted silver spacers

Six silver eye pins

Ten silver head pins

Two 5mm jump rings

Two ear wires

Round nose pliers

Chain nose pliers

Wire nippers

Create these beautiful, on-trend chandeliers and light up your life! Now you can create the same look that is all the rage. The effect is grand, yet the techniques are a snap. You'll have fun creating these dazzling danglers in many different colors.

For each earring

1 Attach a jump ring to an ear wire. String beads as follows onto an eye pin: 4mm round aventurine bead, 5mm silver spacer, 4mm round aventurine bead, 5mm silver spacer, 4mm round aventurine bead. Use round nose pliers to make a loop, then use wire nippers to cut off excess wire. Repeat on another eye pin. Attach one end of each eye pin to the jump ring.

2 String a 6mm round aventurine bead onto a head pin and make a loop above the bead; repeat for another beaded pin (a). String a 4mm round aventurine bead and a cylindrical bead onto an eye pin and make a loop above the cylindrical bead; repeat for another beaded pin (b). String beads onto a head pin as follows: 6mm round aventurine bead, chip, dotted spacer, chip, cylindrical bead (c). Make a loop above the top bead. Set all of the bead pins aside for Step 3.

(See diagram on page 67)

3 Thread one end of an eye pin through a lower loop of one of the eye pins from Step 1. String beads and beaded pins onto the eye pin as follows: 4mm aventurine bead, beaded pin (b), 4mm aventurine bead, beaded pin (c), 4mm aventurine bead, beaded pin (b), 4mm aventurine bead. Thread end of eye pin through lower loop of other eye pin from Step 1, then make a loop. Attach one beaded pin (a) to the loop on each end of the horizontal eye pin.

4 Repeat above steps for second earring.

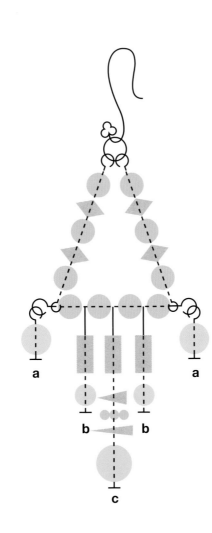

a

a

b

b

c

materials

One piece red leather large enough to accommodate 2 strips for each bracelet. Measure wrist size to determine length of each strip, adding a ½"(1.3cm) overlap. Each strip is ½"(1.3cm) wide.

Sticky Back® Velcro® squares ⅞"(22mm)

Red thread and beading needle small enough to go through beads

Scissors

Rotary cutter and cutting mat

Fabric Glue

Ruler

Beeswax (optional)

Glue

bracelet 1

One red carnelian tube bead

Six red apple coral chips

Two 4mm silver spacer beads

Two 3mm silver spacer beads

Two 2mm silver spacer beads

bracelet 2

Seven red apple coral chips

Seven 2mm silver glass seed beads

red alert

Red is a color that lifts your spirits and adds a spark of excitement to your wardrobe. This trio of leather bracelets are easy to make and comfortable to wear. Add your own favorite beads to make them totally yours—red hot!

Bracelet 1

1 Lay beads out to determine center of band. Knot thread and if desired, run thread through beeswax to make it easier to thread through beads and leather. Bring thread from back, sew on 2mm bead, come back through and sew 3mm bead, and so on until each bead is individually stitched to bracelet. Knot thread, trim and add drop of glue to all stitches. Glue second stip to back side.

Bracelet 2

2 Lay coral chips out evenly across leather band. Beginning at one side, sew from back through hole in chip, string seed bead on and go back through hole in chip. For second chip, with same thread go up through chip, seed bead, and back down. Continue until all are attached and knot on bottom side. Glue second strip to back side.

Bracelet 3

If desired, keep this bracelet plain. Glue two strips together.

3 With scissors cut one Velcro® square (both hook and loop pieces) into quarters. Place hook on one end and loop on other end. Measure on wrist again to assure proper placement before adhering.

materials

beading style: symmetrical, multi-strand with feature bead
finished size: 23"(58.7cm) (not including feature bead)
Note: actual numbers of beads may vary depending on size.

141 4mm fresh water pearls

138 4mm light green jade beads

46 12mm carved jade leaf beads

One 7mm pearl

One 40mm jade feature bead

50 aqua glass seed beads

Beadalon®49 0.33mm beading wire

Beadalon® triple snap clasp

Six silver crimp beads

Beading needle and thread

Chain nose pliers

Glue

cool aqua dream

There is something soft and dreamy about the combination of pearls and aqua colored jade. Embellishing the feature bead with a glass seed bead and pearl tassel adds a touch of sparkle and interest.

1 Cut three 28"(71.4cm) lengths beading wire.

2 On one wire end, thread crimp bead then loop wire through one hole on snap clasp; crimp closed. Repeat with other two wires.

3 String one wire with 138 4mm fresh water pearls. Finish end with crimp bead and attach to other snap clasp. Trim excess wire.

4 String second wire with 4mm jade beads and finish as in Step 3.

5 String third wire with jade leaf beads and repeat finish.

6 For tassel on feature bead: Cut beading thread approximately 12"(30.5cm) and thread needle. String one seed bead on thread, pull end of thread so holes of seed bead are on the side. Loop thread and tie double knot, pulling close to seed bead (diag. a). Add drop of glue to knot. String 7mm pearl, and approximately 35 seed beads, 4mm pearl, one seed bead. Skip last seed bead, insert needle back through pearl and back through 15 seed beads (diag. b).

(See diagram on page 73)

7 Thread through hole in front of feature bead, string one 4mm pearl, four seed beads and loop thread at leaf necklace center, back to front, making sure seed beads are pulled close together, string seven more seed beads and 4mm pearl, bringing string to front of feature bead. Pull thread through hole to back of feature bead, through pearl and seed beads in back. Tie knot at back to secure. Glue knot and push knot into medallion hole. Add drop of glue where thread joins to necklace and on all knots.

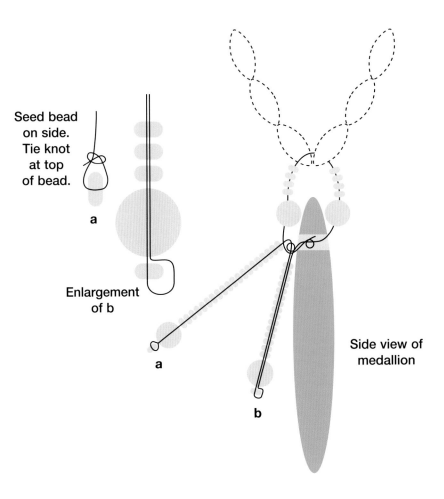

Seed bead
on side.
Tie knot
at top
of bead.

a

Enlargement
of b

a

b

Side view of
medallion

materials

Amounts of beads are approximate.

375 amber glass seed beads

200 red glass seed beads

85 frosted red glass E-beads

65 amber, red, and brown faceted beads in 7mm, 9mm,10mm

Multi-strand silver spacer bars

Beadalon® 49 0.30mm copper color bead stringing wire

Lobster claw clasp

Two 6mm jump rings

12 silver crimp beads

7"(17.8cm) narrow red cotton twill ribbon (optional)

Chain nose pliers

Crimper tool

Glue

This beautiful bracelet is deceptively easy to make. Choosing complimentary colors will add interest to the design. Try adding one color that is slightly unexpected, like the dash of red and purple in this example.

Note

Bead quantities may vary due to bracelet length. Make adjustments accordingly.

1 Determine wrist size and add approximately 5"(12.7cm) for working. Cut three pieces of wire to that size. Wire for seed beads should be approximately 8"(20.3cm) longer than wrist measurement to accommodate twisting.

2 String a crimp bead on wire. Thread one end of wire through second hole on spacer bar. Move crimp bead over wire end, close to spacer bar and crimp with crimper tool. Repeat for remaining two wires, placing one in the middle hole of spacer bar and the other in the sixth hole. The remaining holes will be used for the seed bead strands.

3 String faceted beads on first wire, separating each with red E-beads. End by threading crimp bead on to wire, loop wire through corresponding hole on opposite spacer bar and through crimp bead.

Make sure beads are close enough against the crimp bead and crimp with crimper tool. Repeat above steps for the second and third beaded strands.

4 To string seed beads, repeat step 2 but insert wire through remaining holes on spacer bar. String the crimp bead first and crimp close to the spacer bar. String entire strand with seed beads, and as you go, wrap the strand of faceted beads with seed beads so the seed beads wrap around approximately every two faceted beads. End the strand in the same manner as above and repeat for the remaining two seed bead strands. Adjust twisting as needed. If desired, on back of bracelet, add a drop of glue to places where seed beads meet faceted beads.

5 Attach jump rings and then clasp finding on ends on spacer bars.

6 To create bead tassel: Thread a 7"(17.8cm) strand of wire through the top hole of the spacer bar and knot in center of wire. Add a touch of glue to knot. Feed alternating red and amber seed beads on strand. When tassel is at desired length, end with red E-bead. To lock bead at end, feed wire back through beads beginning at second bead from end. Clip wire and feed through remaining beads. Add a drop of glue at end and where wire ends. Repeat on other tassels.

7 For ribbon tape tassel, choose a complimentary color, such as red. Thread through same hole on spacer bar as beaded tassel, knot. Add one or two beads at each end of ribbon and knot ends. Trim. Place dot of glue on knot. Tie tassels on each end of bracelet.

beading style: symmetrical
finished size (3 strands,
not including feature
bead) 27"(68.8cm)

**45mm carved Chinese
cinnabar feature bead**
(or other bead to your
liking)

**Approx. 162 5mm
garnets (six per inch),
243 3mm garnets (nine
per inch), 272 3mm
faceted emerald green
beads (ten per inch)**
Note: Number of beads
will be determined by
actual size of beads and
desired necklace length.
These numbers are
estimates only.

**One 7mm green glass
bead**

One 9mm red glass bead

**Four 8mm silver spacer
tube beads**

**Six 4mm silver spacer
tube beads**

Six silver crimp beads

**Beadalon® 49 0.33mm
beading wire**

**One 3½"(8.9cm) silver
head pin**

Triple strand snap clasp

Chain nose pliers

asian inspiration

**A striking carved feature bead, lustrous red garnets
and light-catching emerald green faceted beads make
an enchanting combination. This necklace is so easy
to string and so elegant to wear.**

1 Cut three wires approximately 32"(82.4cm) long.
Thread wire with crimp bead, loop through one hole
on snap clasp, slide crimp bead up, crimp closed.
Repeat for other two wires.

2 On first wire, string all 5mm garnets. Attach to other
end of snap clasp as in Step 1.

3 Set aside four green faceted beads. On second wire,
string approximately 126 green faceted beads, 4mm
spacer, four green beads, 4mm spacer, four green
beads, 4mm spacer, four green beads, 4mm spacer,
four green beads, and a 4mm spacer. Continue
stringing remaining green beads to end. Finish end
as in Steps 1 and 2 on other end of snap clasp.

4 On third wire, string approximately 114 3mm
garnets, 8mm spacer, seven garnets, 8mm spacer,
seven garnets, 8mm spacer, four green beads, 4mm
spacer, four green beads and a 4mm spacer.
Continue stringing remaining garnets to end. Finish
on snap clasp as above.

5 To hang feature bead: On head pin string 9mm red
glass bead, 7mm green glass bead, 3mm green bead,
8mm spacer tube, 3mm green bead, feature bead,
3mm green bead, 3mm spacer bead, 3mm green
bead. Hang at center of large garnet strand between
garnets, making a loop in top of head pin.

elegant hair designs

finished size: 8"(20.3cm)

Two wooden chopsticks

Two 2½"(6.4cm) head pins

Assorted beads in complimentary colors and shapes

Small square of fine grade sand paper

Tack cloth

Black acrylic paint and paint brush

Clear acrylic varnish in gloss or matte (as desired)

Small craft drill or awl to make a narrow ½"(1.2cm) deep hole in top of sticks

Glue

There's something very romantic about long silky hair twisted up and accented with hair picks, and these would make welcomed gifts for your long-haired friends. Or, don't paint them and use them as fancy chopsticks!

1 If the tops of sticks have a wider square end, carefully cut off.

2 Lightly sand sticks and round both ends so there aren't any splinters. Wipe sticks with tack cloth. Apply two coats of paint, allowing each coat to dry before applying next coat. Apply varnish and let dry. Lightly sand. Wipe with tack cloth and varnish again. Let dry.

3 Carefully drill a small ½"(1.2cm) deep hole in top of each stick.

4 String beads on eye pin in pleasing design. Start with two small beads at top, graduate to larger bead, then three beads graduating to smaller, leaving ½" to insert pin into stick.

5 Fill hole with glue and insert pin with beads. If needed, add more glue between bottom bead and top of stick. Let dry. Repeat for second stick.

chunky coral twist choker

materials

beading style: multi-strand necklace
finished size: This design is based on a 14" (35.5cm) neck. Total necklace length is 16" (40.8 cm).

300 coral chips (100 per strand)
Vary colors and textures as desired.

Three 18"(45.8cm) strands Beadalon® 19 0.33mm Strand Bead Stringing Wire

Multi-strand silver spacer bars

Six crimp beads

Four 7mm jump rings

Hook and eye clasp

Chain nose pliers

Crimper tool

This red-hot necklace is a cinch to make and will add pizazz to anything you wear. Three strands of coral, each slightly different in texture and color, are gently twisted together to create a stylish sun-kissed statement.

To create this necklace, we used three colors of coral chips. One strand is polished dark red, one is apple coral, and the third is a mixture of dark polished, light polished and apple coral. Measure your neck to determine finished length. Allow for twisting which will shorten slightly. For a 14"(35.5cm) neck, you will need approximately 100 chips per strand. The total necklace length will be approximately 3" (7.5cm) longer once findings are added.

1 Thread one end of beading wire through center hole of spacer bar. Loop and secure with crimp bead. Repeat with second strand through first hole and with third strand through last hole.

2 String one wire with same color chips; the second with the second color and the third alternating three colors.

3 At end, loop three strands through other spacer bar as in Step 1.

4 Add two jump rings to hook and eye clasps and attach on corresponding ends of spacer bars.

5 Trim excess wire and gently twist strands as desired.

hearts and flowers charm bracelet

materials

- **Silver blank charm bracelet with clasp**
- **Four different angel charms**
- **Five 14mm glass hearts in various colors**
- **One 7mm glass star bead**
- **One art glass bead**
- **One small heart button (with two holes)**
- **12 8mm glass hearts in various colors**
- **Six 5mm silver hearts**
- **Glass seed beads and E-beads in assorted colors**
- **Flower shaped shell**
- **Several 4mm round beads such as pearls, garnets, amethyst, glass, silver**
- **18 silver head pins**
- **8mm jump rings**
- **12mm jump rings**
- **The Beadery® 3-in-1 tool**

This bracelet will teach you how to create interesting charms by combining beads and findings. Use your own favorite beads and charms to add a personal touch, and embellish with purchased beads.

1 String the following sets on head pins, finishing each with a loop.

A E-bead, star bead, 14mm glass heart, 8mm glass heart.

B E-bead, 14mm glass heart, seed bead.

C Silver seed bead, art glass bead, E-bead, 8mm glass heart, silver spacer bead, E-bead.

D Silver seed bead, 8mm heart, silver seed bead, 8mm heart, silver seed bead, 8mm heart, silver seed bead. (Each heart a different color)

E Seed bead, colored glass angel bead, seed bead, E-bead.

F 12mm jump ring strung with various colored seed beads and fed through one hole of heart button, 12mm jump ring through second hole of heart button, strung with several colored seed beads.

G Head pin strung with silver seed bead, silver heart, two seed beads, looped and attached to 12mm jump ring.

H Flower shaped shell on 8mm jump ring. On head pin, small silver heart, 8mm heart, 5mm silver heart. Loop head pin and attach to 8mm jump ring, attach to shell flower so they are hanging together. Repeat for a second set in different colors.

I E-bead, 4mm bead, 8mm glass heart, two E-beads, 4mm bead, two E-beads.

J 12mm jump ring strung with seven various colored E-beads and seed beads.

K E-bead, small glass tube bead, seed bead, E-bead, five seed beads.

L 12mm jump ring strung with two silver beads and one pearl.

2 Repeat the following in various color combinations:

   A 5 times

   D 5 times

   B 3 times

3 Repeat other charm sets as you would like.

4 Arrange the charms on the bracelet, joining each charm set to bracelet with a 6mm jump ring.

Assorted sizes, shapes
and colors art glass
beads

Assorted silver spacer
beads

Assorted colors seed
beads

Assorted colors of 2mm,
3mm and 4mm beads

Chain links

Head pins

Eye pins

9mm jump ring

5mm jump rings

Beadalon® 19 Strand
Bead Stringing Wire
0.38mm

Glue

Two ¾"(2.0cm) steel pin
backs

artsy pin-up

This dramatic pin project is a chance to explore your
creativity, pull out all the stops, and let your
imagination soar! Using this idea as inspiration, create
your own. This pin measures 5"(14cm) at the longest
point. You may want to make the dangles shorter.
Consider color and balance when designing your
piece, as well as the size of the person who will
be wearing it.

These lovely chain links joining the beads were taken
from an antique necklace found at a flea market.
There are several options for creating the chains if
you don't have that perfect find: one, loop eye pins
together with beads in between; two, purchase chain
and add beads with jump rings; three, string lengths
of seed beads with larger beads on wire.

Have some creative fun gluing beads on top of beads.
Be sure to use strong glue, such as
Beadalon® G/S Hypo Cement.

(See diagrams on pages 90–91)

Front of large bead

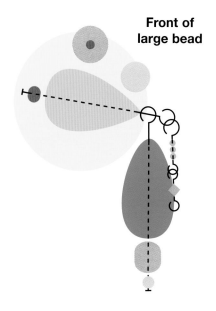

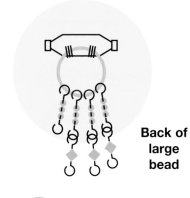

**Back of
large
bead**

**Front of
small bead**

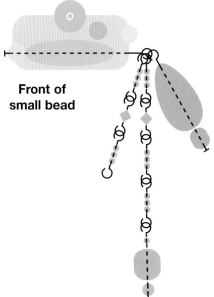

materials

**Measure wrist and cut
ribbons 1½"(38mm) longer.**

**Picot-edged, sheer, ivory
ribbon, 1½"(38mm) wide**

**Gold-edged sheer
ribbon, ¾" (19mm) wide**

**Mauve, satin ribbon
½"(13mm) wide**

**Ivory sheer ribbon, gold
edged ⅜"(10mm) wide**

**⅓ yard (.3m) Heat N'
Bond fusible web**

**Assorted glass seed
beads in pink, lavender,
clear**

**Assorted pearls and
round glass beads in
pink, white, grey, silver,
clear in various sizes
from 3mm to 6mm**

**Assorted novelty glass
beads such as a butterfly,
flowers, hearts**

**Small heart and flower
shaped mother of pearl
buttons**

**Beading needle and
thread**

Sewing needle and thread

Two snaps

Scissors

Iron

Pressing cloth

Fabric glue

E6000® clear glue

ribbons and pearls cuff

Ribbons, pearls and charms create a unique and stylish cuff bracelet you'll love! Rather than stringing beads, you'll be sewing on the ribbon band for a truly feminine one-of-a-kind look. This cuff will look just as wonderful peeking out from the sleeve of your business suit or worn with an evening gown.

1 Cut fusible web strips slightly narrower than each of the ribbons. Fuse the ¾"(19mm) ribbon on top of the widest ribbon. Continue fusing each of the ribbons to each other.

Hint

Place protective paper or cloth on ironing board under the ribbon and on top of ribbon before ironing to prevent webbing glue from getting on board or iron. Repeat this step until all ribbons are fused together.

2 Fold under and press each end of cuff approximately ¼"(.5cm). Fold and press again. Hem stitch edge. Optional: Glue ends with fabric glue instead of hand stitching. Fit cuff to wrist to determine placement of snaps. Sew snaps in place.

3 The beading design is a series of v's across the ribbon. Thread needle with beading thread and knot. Beginning at top edge of one end, sew thread from back to front. String seven seed beads on thread, sew to back side, insert needle at two seed beads back and sew thread through. String seven more seed beads and sew. Bring needle through at the second seed bead back. Repeat chain stitch on entire cuff.

4 The v's are then filled in with pearls, seed beads and other glass beads. See photo, and use your own imagination to fill in. Options: Layer smaller beads on top of larger beads. Either stitch them together, or glue.

5 When finished, dot a small amount of clear glue on knots to secure. Optional: carefully glue a satin ribbon on the back to cover stitches.

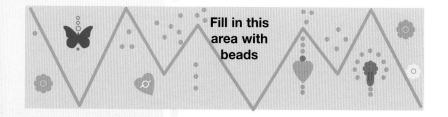

Fill in this area with beads

resources

Beadalon®
205 Carter Drive
West Chester, PA 19382
www.beadalon.com
866-423-2325 for an
authorized Beadalon®
distributor

**The Beadery Craft
Products**
PO Box 178
Hope Valley, RI 02832
www.thebeadery.com

Blue Moon Beads
7855 Hayvenhurst Avenue
Van Nuys, CA 91406
800-377-6715
www.bluemoonbeads.com

Darice, Inc.
13000 Darice Parkway,
Park 82
Strongsville, OH 44149
800-321-1494
www.darice.com

**Beads and Supplies
Online**

www.jewelrysupply.com
Everything from findings
to online lessons.

www.beadz.com
Imported specialty beads
and charms, vintage
German glass.

*www.arizona
beadcompany.com*
Austrian crystal, Peruvian
ceramic pendants.

www.bluesagebeads.com
German, Chinese, Czech,
Italian glass, pearls and
crystals.

beaded jewelry

Editorial Director
Trisha Malcolm

Art Director
Chi Ling Moy

Book Editor
Teri Daniels

Technical Editor
Pat Harste

Designers
Teri Daniels
Katie Hacker
Jackie Ollom

Production Designer
Andrea Grieco

Illustrator
Ryan Brunetti

Manager, Book Division
Michelle Lo

Production Manager
David Joinnides

President and Publisher, Sixth&Spring Books
Art Joinnides